MAGGIE'S BOOK
Memories of Life on Papa Westray

Maggie Harcus MBE

MAGGIE'S BOOK

Memories of Life on Papa Westray

MAGGIE HARCUS

Papay Books
ORKNEY

Published in Great Britain in 2004 by
Papay Books
Hinsobrae
Papa Westray
Orkney KW17 2BU
Scotland

ISBN 0-9549393-0-1

Printed and Bound By
The Orcadian Limited, Hell's Half Acre,
Kirkwall, Orkney, Scotland
Tel 01856 879000: Fax 01856 879000: www.orcadian.co.uk

Contents

Acknowledgements

Writing this book would not have been possible without the generous help of many people on Papa Westray and Westray and others from around the world who checked the details and provided extra information, dates and photos. Thanks are also due to Orkney Islands Council development committee for the grant towards publication costs of the book.

Foreword

This book is about my memories of life on Papa Westray (Papay) spanning 70 years and more. I have been striving to record these memories over the last three years. It was Alan Price who encouraged me to do it. I was telling him all about the way farming was done when I was young and he said 'if you don't write that down it will be lost.' Others have helped me by giving me dates and telling me stories for which I must give thanks.

My interest was farming, although the book has grown to cover many more subjects. There is a complete difference now in the way farming is done compared with my younger days. I have seen many other changes over the years and been involved in them through a number of committees.

I can remember almost every house on the isle occupied and farming their land. The County Show day was the only holiday we got. When I went to the show it featured small tractors and machinery. Now it is quite different with much larger tractors and completely different machinery.

That's called progress. With progress things have certainly changed – some for the better, but others not so good. Travel is much quicker than it used to be but, although there was not much money in the old days, folk seemed more contented then.

I'll conclude by thanking everyone again for their help.

Maggie Harcus,
Midhouse, Papa Westray
November 2004.

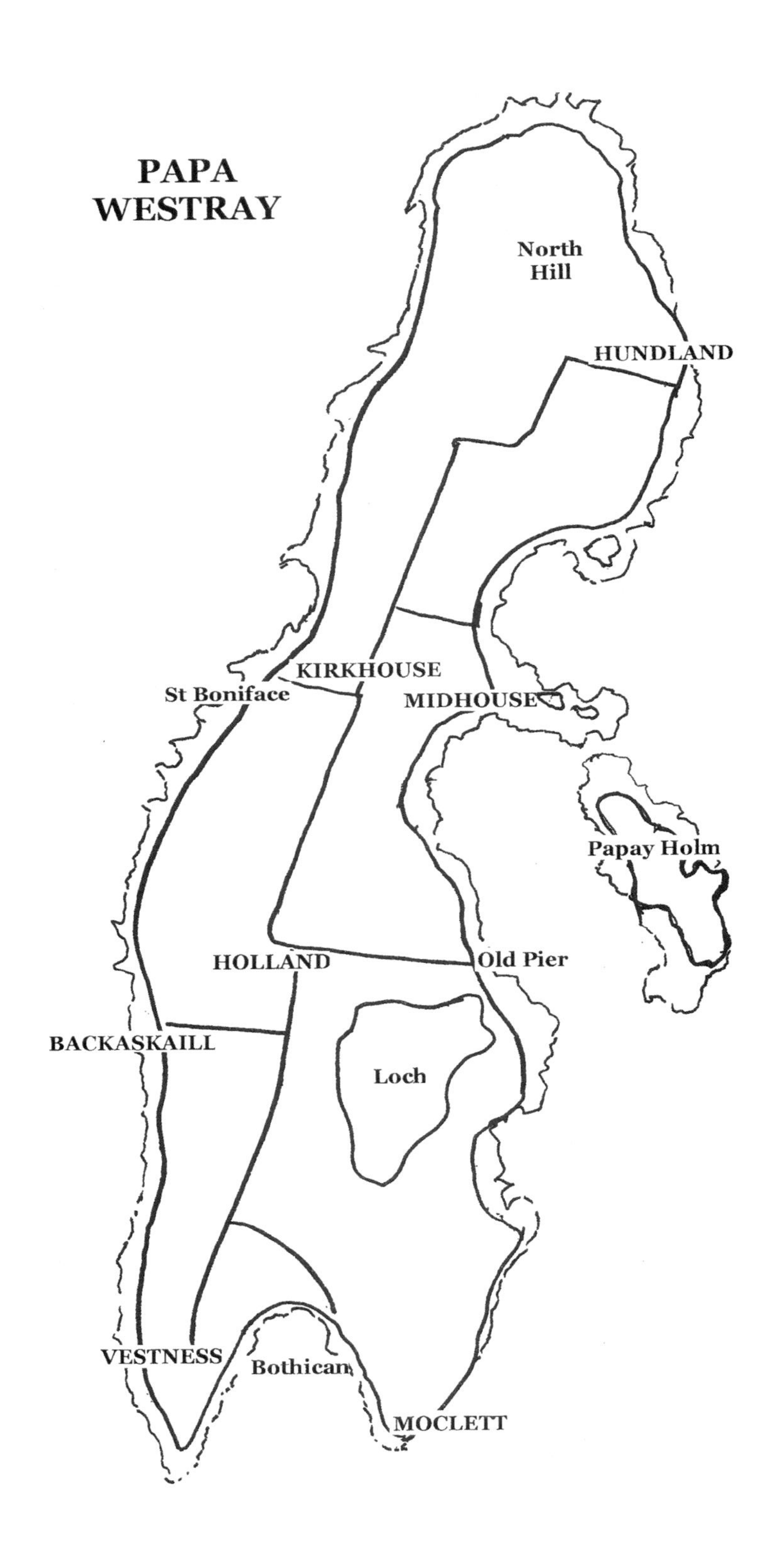
PAPA
WESTRAY
North
Hill
HUNDLAND
KIRKHOUSE
St Boniface
MIDHOUSE
Papay Holm
HOLLAND
Old Pier
BACKASKAILL
Loch
VESTNESS
Bothican
MOCLETT

Maggie, Tommy and Jess Harcus

Growing up on Papay

I was born on the 16th of June 1922 at Midhouse on Papay (Papa Westray) – one of Orkney's northern isles. I have lived in the same house all my life. My parents named me after my grandmother, Margaret Miller. Tommy, my older brother was named after her husband, my grandfather Thomas Harcus. He was born on the 22nd July 1919. My sister Jess was born on the 4th October 1920.

My ancestors have been at Midhouse for a very long time, although my grandfather Thomas (1846-1926) was the first Harcus to live there. He had married my grandmother Margaret Miller (1847-1919) whose family had been at Midhouse since at least the 18th century. Before the present house was built, there was another, 'Old Mithers', Midhoose or Midhouse between Cott and Shorehouse but I don't know what it looked like. The 1841 census shows:

Midhouse No 1 **Miller**

George (born c. 1756) Farmer – my great-great-great-grandfather

Midhouse No 2 **Miller**

David (born 1780) Farmer – my great-great-grandfather
Catherine (born 1784) – my great-great-grandmother
Janet Thomson Female servant

Midhouse No 3 **Miller**

George (born 1813) Fisherman – my great-grandfather
Ann (born 1813) - my great-grandmother
Janet (7)
Ann (6)
John (4)
No Name m (1 month)

The baby with no name was David, who was followed in the next decade by three more children – Catherine, Margaret (my grandmother) and George.

An extension was built on to the present house in 1911 when my father and mother married. That was the last major change. Davie o' Quoys came along one day to Midhouse in the 1920's when we were taking the paper off the walls on the but end. He said he counted 20-fold (layers) o' paper taken off.

I do not remember my grandmother on the Harcus side as she died in 1919, but I remember my grandfather who died in 1926. Grandad spent a lot of time in bed as he had heart problems. I do not remember him going about but when I was be-

My father John D. Harcus, grandad Thomas Harcus, and my brother Thomas Harcus.

ginning to walk, and my mother would be outside working, she would have chairs set at three sides at the front of the bed and, when I got tired, Grandad would take me in bed beside him. He slept in the same box bed in the living room that I use myself to this day. I remember the morning that he died and mind sitting on Maggie o' Cott's knee. On the day of his burial my mother took us into the barn to play while the funeral was going on. Afterwards I was looking for him and wondering where Grandad had gone.

Granny Burgess at Sunnybraes

The other photo is of Granny and Grandad at Sunnybraes' door. Granny was Jessie Burgess (née Ross) and Grandad was Bengi Burgess.

I do not remember Grandad on the Burgess side, as he died in 1923 at Sunnybraes, and I can't mind how long Granny stayed at Sunnybraes before she came to live with us at Midhouse. She had a stroke five years before she died in 1940. Granny was interested in mending clothes and altering garments if they were too big.

I mind on (*remember*) when my sister Jess came with me to take a bottle o' milk to Granny at Sunnybraes one morning and just when we got to the door the bottle slipped out of Jess' hand and broke on the flag at the door. We rushed off to get another bottle o' milk from Auntie Jess at Daybreak to give to Granny.

My mother was good at mending clothes too and did a lot of knitting. She also did a lot of work outside. In those days women did the milking, made butter and cheese and the calves were bucket fed.

If plenty of tangles (seaweed) came ashore my father and mother would be working in them. In Spring, kelp ware would come ashore and it had to be carted and spread to dry. There was something to be done the whole time.

Tommy worked after he stopped school, breaking stones for road metal. In the early 1930's boys were employed to break stones with hammers. The metal was spread on the roads with clay on top. The road surfaces were flattened with heavy blocks of stone that were laid one way one day, taken up at night and then laid the opposite way the following day. He went to work at Holland at the beginning of the Second World War and married Annie from Westray in 1946. Tommy still worked at Holland until they moved to Branstane in Westray on 26th May 1951.

Jess also worked at Holland, as a maid for Willie Traill. She married William Cursiter in 1938 and moved to Charleston. She passed away in 1998.

Maggie's parents in their later years

Auntie Maggie came to stay with us in 1962 and died in 1964. She had been born, also Maggie Harcus, at Midhouse and her husband Tommy Hourston of Vestness had always said that she wanted to go home at the end of her life.

My father died in March 1965 and mother died in February 1967. I have lived alone since.

Papa Westray School as it used to be

School Days

When I started school there was one teacher but I hadn’ been long at school when a second teacher came. Then we wer moved into the peedie (*small*) room. I can’t mind what age w were when I moved back into the big room. There were thirty two youngings at the school when I was a child – all between th ages of 5 and 14.

An article about the school log book says that ‘in 1930 th Inspector had much good to report and praises the work of th Juniors but adds the hint that teacher and pupils should no take school life in too serious a spirit – more brightness is desir able.’

We walked to school. We went to school no matter what th weather was like – we were frightened to stay home. Edith

Sinclair, who was a teacher at Papay school between 1968 and 1982 wrote that:

For all children the school day has always begun with a journey, long or short but what is managed today with speed and even comfort by bike or mini-bus meant for many years a long trudge on foot over rough roads and often through rough weather. (...) Some remembered that fear of the teacher brought children to the school even in bad weather but the Log Books suggest that the weather sometimes overcame that fear.

I can mind one day a morning of sleet. We went as far as Maybo and sheltered there. Davina came oot and said to us youngings: "its no weather tae go to the school" but we went as far as the brae o' Skennist. Jess and me turned back, soaking wet, but Tommie went on to the school.

There were no fences in those days, so we could cross the mire o' Skennist – which was gey (*very*) wet in winter – and over the brae and then along the dyke tae the school. There were patches where the water had raised the earth. We called them boilers – you could still find them at the edge of the loch.

One day we were jumping on what we thought was a boiler – but it turned out to be a beast's belly! The dead beast had been buried but without much earth on top. We soon ran as fast as we could.

Another day we were tormenting the ram, so Tommo o' Skennist came after us. He had a crippled leg and he shouted: "Come leg or I'll leave thee."

The youngings do miss a lot noo-a-days being driven by car but at least they get to school dry, which we were not many a time.

We did not delay going to the school but took longer to get home. We played jumping from one rock to another and sometimes we got our feet wet. One day on the way home some of us, boys and lasses, took a boat fae the pier and went over to the Holm. We did get a telling off when we got home.

We got music lessons but that was during playtime, so I would rather be outside playing than doing the music lessons.

I only got the strap once. We were told by the teacher that we had to be in bed by 8 o'clock. I said that I was not in bed by eight whereas the boys said they were in bed by 8 o'clock (they told me afterwards that it wasn't true). I felt hurt at getting the strap for telling the truth.

Opposite: Papay school c. 1933
Back row: Willie Groat, Frank Flett, Duncan Burgess, Rita Rendall (or Hourston), Nellie Burgess, Peggie Harcus, Henry Rendall, Tommy Groat, James Hourston.
Second Row: Isabel Rendall, Maggie Harcus, Bessie Laughton, Jean Burgess.
Front row: David Hourston, John Rendall, Tommy Mackay, Alex Davidson, Billy Groat, Kathleen Drever, Mina Hourston, Ian Rendall, George Willie Rendall, Jimmy Burgess.
Teachers: thought to be Miss Anderson and Miss Laird.

There were no school dinners then, often we went to Auntie at Daybreak for a piece and cocoa. *Miss Sinclair described 'pieces' as a 'slight substitute for a midday meal' that most commonly were thick bannocks of bere meal.*

The teacher had a desk with a platform where her chair stood. She got mad many a time but one day she was VERY mad. The leg of her chair slipped off the platform and she fell. After that, the platform was cut away from the desk.

Her desk stood near where the fire was and she liked the heat. If you were near the front you could find the warmth but if you were in the back row there was not much heat.

We used slates for writing on which had to be cleaned. The usual way was to spit on the slate and clean it wi' your sleeve. Some might have a small bottle o' water and a rag – it was more hygienic than spitting on it. When we got older we would use pen and ink.

We had school concerts and Christmas parties. Also we had Guides and Brownies and we would light a camp fire and cook tatties (*potatoes*) and sausages. They were good fried on a fire outside.

One day the lum (*chimney*) went on fire so we got the remainder of the day off. I remember my brother Tammie coming home and throwing his school bag in the bed saying "The lum's gaen on fire!"

We always had a picnic when the school closed for the summer holidays. We might get a tub of ice cream but it nearly melted as there were no freezers then. We would have a Sunday School picnic and I can mind Jamie Phillips the lay preacher coming wi' a big bag of worded sweeties (*conversation lozenges*). He threw them out on the grass and there was a scramble to see how many sweeties we could get.

The day I sat my leaving certificate was a right cold day and I had been getting teeth out the day before, so I was not feeling very good. That might have been the reason why I did not get very high marks.

Westray from the south of Papay in Winter

Christmas and Hogmanay

Nowadays, turkey is the main dish on Christmas Day – we never had heard of turkey when I was young. In those days Christmas dinner was a roast of beef or maybe a hen. An older cow would have been butched for Christmas and sold. A cheap dinner could have been had at a shilling a pound for a roast or sixpence a pound for boiling.

We sent a Christmas box to my Aunt and Uncle in Leith (*near Edinburgh*). They had six girls. The box contained pork, puddings, a hen, butter, cheese and, likely, Christmas presents and a bere bannock or two. When the box came back it was a great day as it was filled with a variety of things: apples, oranges, dates and a currant bun, Christmas presents and clothes that the girls had outgrown.

Christmas and New Year were celebrated quite differently from today. Christmas Day we would go visiting to Vestness and other houses in the south end of the isle. Christmas night and New Year's night there would be a dance in the school. Tom Hourston from Whitelooms and Dannie Mackay o' Maybo were the musicians on the fiddle with Willie Cursiter (Charleston) on the button key accordion.

Before the Second World War we would meet at the shop at Backaskaill to take in the New Year – there was not much first-footing done then-a-days. In 1953, when Ian Young was the teacher on Papay he started the Watch Night Service at the Kirk and that was where we took in the New Year. This tradition continues today.

There was a fairly large congregation at the first Watch Night Service and Mr and Mrs Young invited everyone to come to the Schoolhouse for a cup of tea after the service. It was a very rainy night and everyone's feet were muddy. We then went first footing. Coming past the Schoolhouse about 5 o'clock in the morning the lights were on as they were still cleaning up after the folk had all left.

When the old Earl Thorfinn or Sigurd (*inter-island steamers*) were on the go one of them would be lying at the Gill Pier, Westray as a number of the crew were Westray men. They would blow the siren to take in the New Year.

New Year's Day was spent visiting Auntie Maggie and Uncle Tammie of Vestness would come along.

Lots of visiting was done during the winter and it was pleasant when it was moonlight as mostly everyone was walking. Nowadays with fewer folk on the island there's not much visiting done and with the TV in the corner you are likely to watch it. We did not have that attraction long ago.

John David Harcus and horses, late 1930s

Farming on Papay

Life on Papa Westray seventy years ago bears no comparison to what it is today. The number of people on the island then was 247. I can remember all the houses being occupied and each was a farm. Some houses had two families living in them. Holland was the biggest farm and had three cattlemen and three horsemen. Holland also employed women for milking the coos (*cows*).

Cattle

We had three coos and their followers and we bought an extra calf so that we had four to sell. Before I stopped farming, I increased to four coos and their young. In the old days, the beasts were all on tether. They were put to the clover in the morning and in the afternoon were taken to the well for water and then tethered on the natural grass. After the Second World War fencings were put up and the beasts were then put loose. The coos were milked morning and night and the calves bucket fed. Later (about 1959) the calves were put on the coos to suck for themselves. One coo was hand-milked for our own use so that calf was still bucket fed.

Anna Margaret Harcus wearing a sackiebrat c. 1950

The beasts got a varied diet of hay, straw, chaff, neeps and nuts to give as a feed. Nowadays it's all silage, crushed barley and minerals. First in the morning the beasts got a feed of straw. We would then have our breakfast. Afterwards the coos were milked and the byre cleaned. The milking coos were kept in every night so the byre was not very easy to clean - it was a job to get the dung to stay on the barrow. The coos were gey dirty: a sackiebrat (an apron made out of a Hessian sack) was required and an auld jacket. The beasts then got a feed of neeps and chaff or hay. After dinner another feed of neeps and they were watered with buckets and a further feed of hay. Then, after teatime, they would get their supper of straw. The evening milking was done before that and the byre would be cleaned again.

Winter weather was more severe then-a-days than it is now: much more snow and frost. Buckets of water were carried from the well for the beasts and I have seen icicles hanging from our jackets before we would reach the byre. When the beasts first went outside in the springtime they were only oot for a short time then taken in. This was done for a few days until they got accustomed to the grass.

Cattle dealers would come and buy the beasts. Tammie Mason Mason could tell by looking at a beast what girth it was. If a beast was 6 feet it was a big beast. Afore the days when Tammie Mason and David Spence were the cattle dealers, the beasts were sold to Holland farm. My father was a hairst (*harvest*) hand at Holland. Afore the hairst was finished, the feeding byre at Holland was filled. I think it held 24 beasts. They would get plenty of organic feed: hay, straw, neeps and bruised oats. These beasts were ready for selling after Christmas.

Milk and cheese

When first I mind, the milk was placed in basins and the cream rose to the top. It was put in a jar and when full it was then kirned (*churned*) and made into butter. In the summer, when there was plenty of milk, cheeses were made. They were very good. Later, we had a separator so that did away with the basins.

Cheese needed a bucket of milk that was heated before a teaspoon of rennet was added. When the curds were ready the curds were broken and when it was set together it was put in a cheese press and left for a couple of days. It could be eaten when new or dried - both very good. When dry, the cheese was put in oatmeal and the outside got hard so it kept longer.

Pigs

Most houses would rear a pig for their own use. They were fed on boiled tatties and skim milk or cheese whey. In harvest time a couple of buckets of tatties would be dug every morning to be boiled for the hens and pig. When the pig was older it would also get some oatmeal. It would be nine or ten months old before it was butched. The day the pig was killed the boiler had to be filled wi' water and a fire lighted. When the water was nearly boiling more cold water had to be added to get the correct heat for scalding off the hair. The pig was usually killed on a day in December and it took most of the daylight before all the work was finished.

The pig was then hung for a couple of days. It would be cut down and our neighbour would get a piece of pork. When their pig was killed we would get a piece of theirs. A fresh piece of pork was good when fried with onions.

Maggie and the Midhouse pig

Springtime

Plooing (*ploughing*) was done with a horse and one or two beasts. The picture shows a horse and two beasts harrowing. I remember we had a cow and a horse working together. The cow was milked and fed in the morning and then did the morning yoke. It was taken home at dinner time and got another feed and then worked another yoke. It was milked once more at night and given another feed. It was watered twice a day by bucket. Drinking bowls were put in the byre in 1964 and what an improvement.

The oats or bere were sown by hand in the first half of the twentieth century, markers being set up and moved two and a half paces each time. Sowing might be done using both hands and a sowing sheet. Alternatively, some folk used one hand and a bucket. Sacks of grain were spaced at appropriate distances along the length of the field.

The dung was forked from the middens into a cart and a two-toed pick used to pull it off in rows on the land. This was spread over the field – again with the fork - and then plooed into the ground.

Ware was also carted on the land and spread and plooed in the same backbreaking way. It was put on where the corn was grown and also the tatties. Farming was truly organic in those days.

John David Harcus harrowing at Midhouse, 1930s

Tattie planting

This was also done by hand with an acre of tatties planted. A shallow drill was made and dung was sparked in the drill and spread. The tatties were planted and then covered by the horse and drill ploo (plough). After the Second World War the tattie planter was used. This was much easier. When the tatties were big enough, they were hoed. When it was time to take the tatties up, the drill ploo was used to ploo drills. A four-toed pick was used to scrape the drills and the tatties gathered. Buckets of tatties were emptied into baskets which were, in turn, emptied into the cart. Later, when we had a tattie digger, that method was still used but the tatties were emptied into sacks.

During the war we got a subsidy for the tatties – I can't mind how much an acre – and some did take advantage and planted the tatties a good distance between so as to cover more ground. The varieties planted were: Arran Banner, Midlothian, Arran Chief, Irish Queen, Up-to-date, Duke of York, Creamy Blossom, Golden Wonder, Record and Dunbar.

Neep sowing

Neep sowing was done by a machine. When they were big enough, they were singled and later hoed by hand. During winter, the neeps were carted home and fed to the beasts. In the springtime, when plooing was done, the cart would be left in the land and filled and the load taken home at dinner time.

Jimmy Hourston and Tom Hourston loading manure at Vestness c. 1950

Hay making

Long ago, before the horse and reaper were used, hay woul have been cut by a scythe. The hay was then turned with a for and, when dry enough, it was raked into rows and spread the coled (piled into small stacks on the field) to get it perfectly dry Then it was coled again before being taken into the yard an built into a long stack. Later we made round stacks. In winte the hay was tied in windlins to feed to the beasts. A windlin wa an armful of hay or straw tied with its own ends.

Time moved on and the hay was turned with a hay turne and baled with a baler, still heavy to get it in and lift in a stac or put in houses.

Harvest

By the time the hay was finished it was nearly time to start the harvest work. Again the crop would have been cut with the scythe before the horse and reaper were used. The sheaves had to be lifted and a band put around them and then stooked. When the sheaves were dry they were taken into the yard and built in stacks. Wintertime the sheaves were taken into the barn and thrashed; the straw was tied in windlins and also fed to the beasts.

Anna Margaret Harcus stoking sheaves, Midhouse, 1940s

Until about 1930 the threshing was done by a windy gear. Sails were put on to drive the mill. Later an engine was used. Before Holland had an engine, horses were used to drive the mill. The mill tramp is still there.

At the sale at Holland in 1922 there was a binder. I remember going wi' my father and mother to see a binder working at

The tractor age

Holland. The binder was pulled by three horses. Whether that was a new binder they had I can't mind on but it was great to see the sheaves thrown out already tied. The first binder we had was in 1950 when we had the first tractor. The binder was shared with Kimbland. Before that we had a horse reaper and then a two-horse reaper and Kimbland and us cut together in the harvest time.

The oats and bere grain were put to Westray or Stronsay and when those mills stopped grinding the grain was put to the Ayre Mills, Kirkwall. The meal was packed hard by foot: either you would put on clean stockings or wash your rubber boots clean to pack the meal.

Willie Kirkness making a chair back

Making Chair Backs

My father made backs for Orkney chairs during the winter months. This gave the men something to do during winter. The pay was not great but a bit extra was always useful. My father made big sized backs for which he would get 5 shillings in old money, but this had risen to 12 shillings and 6 pence shortly before he stopped making them.

The bands were made of raffia and I remember winding the bands. Two chair backs were sent away at a time and when the sack came back there was enough raffia inside to keep him working until another two were ready for shipping to D.M. Kirkness. The backs were made in a chair frame and cut out.

Gloy (*drawn straw*) for making the chair backs was made by putting the grain end of the sheaf in the threshing mill and then pulled back to take the grain off. Black oat straw was the best for the backs.

A back made by my father was put in a chair that was presented as a wedding gift from Orkney to King George VI and Queen Elizabeth.

Baiting lines c. 1930, Papay. Andrew Groat, John David Harcus and John Foulis.

Fishing

I remember my father and Jamie o' Hinso going haddock fishing. Most of the men went fishing. Usually my father fished with John o' the Green and Andrew o' Kimbland. Skiffs were the kind of boat that I mind, about 16 feet long, a big sail but no engine. My father had a boat named 'Dewdrop'. The boat was tarred inside and painted blue and red outside. It was anchored off the shore with a small dinghy to get to it. It was brought in and kept in a naust during the winter. *Nausts are stone-lined boat-shaped shelters dug into the ground above the tide line.* There used to be a big deep naust on the banks but it has mostly washed away. I was only once or twice at the haddock fishing. Once I went out as far as Moclett with my father.

The haddock line was baited with lugworms or limpets. If the tide was low in the early morning, the lugworms would be dug out and the long line baited ready to go off in the afternoon. The limpets came from the rocks below Cott. They would take the line out with the boat, sink one end and attach the other to a buoy. Sometimes the line would be set between the land and the Holm and they would catch flounders. Nowadays they would use a shorter line, perhaps just six hooks with lugworms, put over the side for catching cuithes.

When they came ashore the fish would be divided in two lots and either me or my sister would turn our backs. My father would point to one lot and we had to say who got that lot. We were quite young and did not like to say that it was our father's lot. Mother would have the pot boiling and the fish would be cleaned and boiled right away for supper.

Salting the haddock

The rest of the fish would be made ready next day for salting. Big haddock were split but most were usually salted whole. The fish were put in layers in a tub and salt placed between each layer – that made the pickle. They were left in the pickle for up to a week and then taken out and pressed to take some of the pickle away. Then they would be laid out to dry. When dry enough they were taken in, tied in pairs and put up in the roof to dry until they were ready for eating.

A salt haddo' and tatties and dippings made a good tasty dinner. The haddock were soaked overnight and boiled. The water was changed once to take the salt away. 'Dippings' were melted butter or margarine.

Cuithes and silocks

Cuithe (*Coley*) fishing was very popular and I have hauled many a score of cuithes. Cuithes or silocks, as they were called when they were small, could be hauled at the rocks: Hertigoe and Chestie, the rocks west o' Kimbland. The wands would be baited with raw limpets taken off the rocks. Some of the older men would chew the limpets and spit them into the water to attract the cuithes. I think my father may have done that – and Andrew Groat of Kimbland. In earlier days silocks could be caught in a net.

West shore of Papay

The cuithes could be caught with either nets or baited wands. They were good during the May flood but they would come earlier than that. Cloudy days were best. There were three hooks on each wand. The wands were hollow, like bamboo. They were about 6 ft long and each man would hold three wands from the boat. Willie Hewison of Shorehouse was good at catching them from the boat.

My granduncle Stewart Harcus would come to the north end to go off to the cuithes wi' my faither. One night someone put a heavy stone in the bottom of his cubbie (*straw bag*) and filled it with cuithes on top and the old man carried it on his back to Southhouse about two mile away. The stone was at Southhouse back door for many years after and may still be there.

Cuithes were good fried or boiled when salted and dried. We also hung them outside with no salt until they were dry. They had a sour taste but were good with a good tattie – it made a tasty and cheap meal.

Silocks could be soured by putting them in a container with straw. They were pressed and were very good when fried but gey strong and sour. You needed to acquire a taste for them.

Cockles and spoots

You could find a few cockles on the spoot sand, which was exposed on the ebb tide. They were boiled same as spoots (razorfish), maybe with some vinegar. Spoots could be cooked in different ways. Mima o'Cott cooked them in the oven with milk. If you fried them in a pan you had to keep them moving and cook for only a few minutes. I didn't like whelks so much.

Creeling

I went to the creels sometimes wi' father. We only creeled in the summer and would have about twenty or thirty creels, but

Creels at the old pier

not on a backrope. A backrope had a dozen or more creels on We had just single creels. We caught lobsters that were sold to a Kirkwall merchant. We did not eat them ourselves although I have tasted them. I was never keen on anything but the white meat from the big toes – the same for crabs as well.

Nowadays, they creel all the year when the weather is suit-able. They will have about 200 creels in the good weather – maybe fewer in winter.

Kelp burning on Papa Westray

Kelp making

Plenty of tangles came ashore. One year my father and mother had a hundred cartloads of tangles taken up afore Christmas. The tangles were built in piles to dry and when we were going to the school we would shelter at the tanglie pile.

The ware was carted in the springtime and spread out on the grass to dry. It grew grand grass where the ware had been spread. The tangles and ware were burned in a kelp kiln. The kiln was a hole in the ground with slates set around the sides. When burning tangles and ware had gone on all day the kiln would be full of kelp. It was beaten together and next day it was hard. It was then dug out and carted tae the store and weighed. When the coal boats came with coal they would take a load o' kelp away.

Working kelp ware

The last kelp was in the store for a long time but was eventually carted out and spread on the east road. When coming home from the school we had great fun running through the reek from the kiln burning along the shore.

Willie o' Cott was carting kelp tae the Store. So on the east road he was going wi' his load and Johnnie o' Hinso was coming towards him wi' an empty cart. There's no laybye's on that road so the horses came face to face and Johnnie o' Hinso said "thou doon me this time Willie".

The kelp was paid for in weighs - a weigh is 500kg. The laird had to get his share of the kelp money and it did not leave much for the folk who did the work. There was a court case atween the laird and the folk. The Sheriff wanted the folk to say that the laird forced them to make so much kelp but one man said they would make as little or as muckle as they liked. After the farms were bought, the laird would not have the claim on the kelp money.

There were various things taken out of the kelp but it was found that it could be cheaper to get it from other sources. That was one reason why the kelp making was stopped. When making the kelp by burning the ware and tangles was stopped, the tangles were gathered and dried and when dry they were tied in bundles and weighed. The price was good for the tangles. That went on for a number of years but now they are not taking the tangles.

Steps at the old Kelp Store

Snowfall in recent years does not compare with 1947

Hens, Snow and Hurricanes

Egg production was once a major activity on Papay Every house would have 70 to 80 hens, some maybe more There were so many henhouses on the land with their dark roofs that one old gentleman said 'it was a tarred road to the Kirk. There was an agricultural cooperative society and they collected and shipped the eggs. Andrew Miller of Daybreak collected the north end and John Cursiter of Charleston the south end. During the Second World War eggs were dear. After the war we shipped hens – three in a bundle. We got 7 pounds 3 shillings and 7 pence for nine hens.

Hens got a feed twice a day. Nettles were boiled and mixed with the hen feed – boiled tatties and meal. When the crop was taken in the hen houses were put out on the stubbles. The hens would hunt and find grain that had fallen out of the sheaves. The result was good free-range eggs.

Hens when they clucked would be set on eggs. The eggs might be cosed (*exchanged*) from another house. Usually hens would be set on duck eggs and by the time they were hatched the hen would be getting gey tired as duck eggs took four weeks to hatch. When the ducklings grew bigger the hen would be tethered and the ducks would wander away from them to fend for themselves.

Hens would also be tethered when they had chicks. When the chicks were small, a run would be made for them. It was made of fine-meshed wire nailed to a wooden frame.

Snow in 1947

There was a big snow in 1947. It started early in February and it was nearly the end of March before it was all away. The hens were kept in for a time but the snow lasted so long we let them oot. The hen houses were on the land, the weather was bonnie, so the hens came to meet you walking on top o' the snow.

The roads were all blocked and had to be cleared with shovels – no tractors or diggers then. Big blocks of snow lay at the sides o' the road like the concrete blocks at the barriers, but the snow eventually melted away.

We did get a lovely summer that year.

Hurricanes

The first hurricane was in January 1952. I was a bit scared – it was gey noisy with the wind sounding like someone screaming. Nobody got hurt and our animals were alright though some slates blew off the roof. The boats were in the nausts and tied down so most of them survived. Stacks were also blown over and some of those blew on the sea.

However, the henhouses were smashed and some blown on the sea. There was one floating past Moclett point and the hens were heard cackling. There was a fearful loss as so many hens got killed. My neighbours at the Green had four henhouses out on the land and I can mind, when the daylight got bright enough that I could see, the henhouses were all flattened. Most of the hen houses were made of wood. They would have been about 6’ by 8’ and tied down to take the force of normal winds. In the few stone buildings the hens survived.

A second hurricane happened on January 31st 1953. It was during the day. The Earl Thorfin left Kirkwall that morning and was heading for Stronsay when the steering gear broke. The crew had to steer by hand, taking turns and they had to run before the wind. I had gone to Westray the day before (Friday) because it was a bonny day. My brother was farming at Branstane. I stayed the night there. We were all wondering what had happened to the Thorfin – a good few of the crew belonged to Westray. That night we could not go to bed until we found out. For hours no one knew where they were but late that Saturday night word came that they had reached Aberdeen. There were not many phones in those days, so we only knew when somebody came along and told us the Thorfin was safe, lying off Aberdeen.

Owing to the wind, the harbour was closed so they could not get alongside until the wind moderated.

Anna of Charleston was staying with my father and mother because I was away. She was about fifteen years old. She had diabetes and took the measles 2 years later and died.

Waiting at the old pier, 1914

Steamers, Piers and Goods

The boat came from Kirkwall on Wednesday and Friday. I stayed in Westray on Wednesday night and came along Thurs day morning. It came into the pier every second week and wen along the other islands on the way back into Kirkwall. On Fri days the steamer did the round trip. On Saturdays the boa came to the pier every second week.

On the days when the steamer did not come to the pier a small boat would go out and would take all kinds of cargo or board. If the boat was going off at Bothican a flag was hoisted a Charleston to let the steamer's crew know where to stop. If no flag was put up this meant that the small boat was coming off a Backaskaill.

A horse and cart came alongside the small boat to take the goods on to the beach. There was a jetty at Backaskaill where the passengers could get ashore. At Bothican the boatmen carried the passengers ashore.

Rowing out to the steamer at Bothican

On Saturdays, when the steamer came to the pier, the breadbox would be taken up to the end of the store. It was a wooden box. Lots of people would be there to get their loaves. There were no pan or sliced loaves then. If you had a message bag the two loaves would be put in the bag – no wrapped loaves then either. If you did no have a bag the two loaves would be carried home under your arms.

Davie Groat at Backaskaill would have fresh mutton at the weekend – he butched lambs. There would be beef ordered from Kirkwall for the middle o' the week. We would also have cockie chickens: very good stewed. For breakfast it was always gruel (*porage*) made from our own oats ground into meal. In fact our living was very organic.

Steamer at the old pier

Coal delivery

The Papay Agricultural Co-operative Society had a cargo of coal and W.F.M. Brown of Holland also had a cargo of coal When the coal boats were unloaded they would take a cargo of kelp with them – that was in the days when kelp was made of course. It would be in the early 1930s when the smaller boats would take a cargo of kelp away. Later, when bigger boats came the coal would be divided between Papay and North Ronaldsay.

The coal was moved by horse and cart. Some horses were frightened by the loading process. The horses used for coal carting would be loosed and yoked into the other cart and would take the load from the ship. It would be unyoked and the other horse would be yoked into the cart in its place. In the early 1950s tractors and trailers were used and the coal would be delivered to anyone who wanted it.

Unloading at Backaskaill

Four men would be in the hold shovelling coal in the barrels and one man tipping them in the cart or the trailer. The coal was shovelled into barrels. If it was the smaller barrel that was used for the horse cart it could be two barrels to make a load. Another man would keep note of the loads and tell the tractor driver what house he had to go to. We usually took a year's supply from the boat – it was cheaper taking it in quantity. There was plenty stored on the isle so we could get more if we did not have enough.

George Burgar with the mail at Backaskaill, early 1900s

Shops on Papay

The first shop that I mind was in a peedie room in Bayview. It was in a small closet between the but end and the ben end, roughly where there is a small bedroom now. There were shelves and, I think, a counter. Robbie Rendall and his wife Mary ran the peedie shop. Most groceries would have been sold in the shop but what has kept it so clear in my mind is the memory of Jess my sister and me going there for two enamel soup plates. They were white with a blue edge.

In fact, there were three shops on the isle at one time:

* One at Tredwall run by Geordie Rendall and his wife Katie after the one they closed at Bayview. That might have been 1929 or early 1930.

* Geordie Drever's in School Place.

* Groat and Miller at Backaskaill.

Geordie Rendall, peedie Robbie Rendall and fat Robbo Rendall had a boat in which they went to Kirkwall for goods. And I mind Geordie Rendall going round wi' a van – it was a motor van. That would have been in the early 1930s.

Geordie Drever's shop at School Place was in a room in the hoose, and much bigger than the one at Bayview. So there was more variety in Geordie's shop. He had the first wireless on Papay and when you were at the shop he wanted you to come in and listen to the wireless through earphones.

He had the shop when I was going to the school. One thing I had on my mind then was buying 'Oggie Poggie Eyes' – big sweeties – eight for an old penny. They lasted a good while and as you sucked them the colour changed. We did not get much pocket money in those days and it was usually spent on sweeties. We never had more than a penny or two pence to spend. One day when I came to Daybreak for my cocoa and bread Auntie thought my face was swollen. But I was sucking on a big Oggie Poggie Eye. That would have been about 1930.

Geordie Drever had a horse van that he went around the island with. He would take a neep out of the pile and give it to the horse to eat while we were getting our messages. One day the

Shop van at Nouster

wheel came off the cart and an old man said that there was more money in the midden o' the Ness than at Klondyke.

School Place was vacant for a time after Geordie Drever died Willie Rendall and his parents moved there and Willie started a shop. It was much bigger than in Geordie's time. Willie's father died in 1955 and Willie left the following year. Then Jim Rendall came home from doing his National Service. Jim and his mother kept the shop going for a time but they found it was not paying.

Jim went to Backaskaill in 1959 to work for Davy Groat and then his wife Lena after Davy died. She moved to Kirkwall and Jim and Margaret kept the shop, until again they found it was not making a profit. After this Highlands and Islands came in and the first Co-op was started. The Papay Community Co-op was opened in 1980.

Wartime

The Second World War started on the 3rd of September 1939. It was a miserable day, weather wise, and a sad day to think Britain was at war. I was 17 years old and I was home at Midhouse with my father and mother and Tommy my brother. We had a wireless and heard it announced that Britain was at war. I don't mind so clearly about VE day.

We had to get blackout shutters on the windows and sky-light. Food was rationed but we were well-off in that respect, having our own stuff growing and cows milked. So we had plenty of milk, butter, cheese and also eggs. Eggs were dear and scarce during the war and a plane would come for them. The plane usually landed in a field of Holland's and the men would come and ask for eggs. The officials would not know the men were getting eggs on the quiet.

Rhubarb grew in abundance on the island, as it still does. For once we got a market for this. Davie Groat at Backaskaill bought the rhubarb and he sent it to the troops in Orkney. There were a lot of men stationed in Orkney during the war.

The north hill in wartime

In 1942 the Navy took over the North Hill for a practice shooting range and targets were put up on the hill. The Coast-guard crew had kept watch day and night from the watch hut at Ereval but, when the hill was taken over, the watch hut was moved to Hindgreenie. This gave the men much better conditions in which to go out in the dark than having to go over the hill to Ereval – they were not supposed to use a light. One night a light was seen on the hill and the officials phoned asking i they should fire at the light. But the coastguard were told to in vestigate first. It turned out to be Danny o' Maybo using a ligh walking out to Ereval.

When the shooting was on there were men in dugouts di recting the guns. But the warships could be rolling in the swel and every shell did not land on the hill. We had eight naval me altogether, with two staying at any one time. The seaplan landed in the bay and taxied into the pier to land the men. Th men stayed at different houses, mostly in the north end of Papa while the officers stayed at Cott.

The two coming to stay with us were told to go to the hous with the green door. They stayed only a couple of nights an then another two would come. There were two who staye longer as it was not weather for the seaplane to pick them up. still keep in touch with one of the men. He was one of the tw who were here when a shell landed near our house and killed beast belonging to our neighbour Mrs Hewison at Shorehouse The boys came from the south of England to Papay, did thei time in the dugouts and, when they left Papay, went back to th south of England and were in the D-Day landing. Ian Greig wen across to France in the morning, got shrapnel in his shoulde and was back in Britain in the evening. I asked Ian about hi memories. This is what he wrote:

"It is now 60 years ago this year since I was one of th Forward Observation Bombardment Units who was billete with your mother and father and yourself at Midhouse. N doubt you will be able to tell about as much as I can as you

were as much in the firing line as I was at the bombardment of the North Hill.

"Being such a long time ago I have to stretch my memory although episodes like that leave a lasting memory in one's self. What I can recall was being a R.N. Telegraphist and part of the Forward Operating Bombardment Unit operating, in my case, from the battleships 'Nelson' and 'King George V', which I was serving in for a short time while in Scapa Flow. We were put ashore in Papa to do rehearsing for the landings for D-day. As wireless operators our job was to direct the ships' fire on to specific targets. No doubt at some point the direction of fire went astray and, as you will know, one of your neighbours got a near miss and, I believe, killed one of the animals.

"I'm sure the residents of Papa Westray would take some pride in the winning of the war from the fact they helped so much in the preparation of D Day. As you know I was in the first wave of troops to land on 'Sword Beach' with the Kings Own Light Infantry to give them support until they got their own guns ashore. Unfortunately I was wounded in the initial landing and spent one year in hospital with a compound fracture of the Humerus and severed radial and median nerves to my left arm. (...)"

After the beast was killed, folk staying in the north end had to leave the houses at night if the ships were going to shell. There were two nights when we were told to go but on both occasions no shelling was done. The first night, my father and mother went to Daybreak and I went to the school with a lot more people. The army sent a pile of blankets and we lay on the floor and didn't get much sleep. The second night my mother and me went to Daybreak. Father didn't go. We had two of the boys leaving in the morning so father said he would stay and make breakfast for them.

If shelling was done during the day, a flag went up to let us know that we were to stop plooing if the horses were working – this was not to frighten the horses.

Letters in wartime

Letters were censored during the war. My mother had sent a small parcel to my cousin saying that it was a 'small minding.' The censors sent a note to my cousin – which she sent on to my mother – saying it had been noted that she had utilised parcels for the purpose of smuggling messages past the censorship! My mother said it wasn't a Scotsman who censored that letter or he would have known what a small minding meant.

Travelling between the isles

The steamer came on Saturday and called at the old pier. It stayed in Westray over the weekend and sailed on Monday morning, calling at Papay, Eday, Sanday and Stronsay then on to Kirkwall. In summer I think they came again on Tuesday, around the islands. This service carried on after the war. There were no trip days then. A drifter came with passengers some days.

The timetables were made out with the nicknames of the islands. They would be leaving Auks, calling along Dundies, then Scarfs, then Gruelly Belkies and Limpets and on to Starlings. When the steamer came by the west isles they would leave

Starlings (Kirkwall), then go to Whelks (Wyre) and Mares (Rousay) and Burstin-lumps (Egilsay).

Papay folk in the war

Robbie Hume (Newhouses) and Willie Groat (Kimbland) were in the Royal Navy. There were a few boys in the Merchant Navy. I can mind some of them: Davie Flett – his ship was torpedoed; Henry Rendall; George Rendall (Tredwall) – he was torpedoed and was in a lifeboat along with other crew members for nearly two weeks; Stewart Groat (Ness) – he was torpedoed more than once; Johnny Burgess (South Via); Duncan Burgess (South Via) – his ship was torpedoed. Stewart Groat of Kimbland was lost during the war. He fell down the hold of a boat.

Service at the War Memorial

The *Bellavista* aground

The *Bellavista*

On 29th July 1948 the *Bellavista* went ashore on Mull Head on Papay. There was fog and the coastguard on watch could not see that there was a ship ashore.

The coastguard phoned from Kirkwall that there was a ship ashore, either on Mull Head on Papay or Mull Head on Deerness, so the man on watch had to walk until he could see if there was a ship, but the ship was ashore.

The coastguard crew was called out but the men did not want to leave the ship then, and other ships came to see if they could help to tow the *Bellavista* off. When the fog cleared it was a bonny day, but at the weekend the weather worsened and the crew was taken off by breeches buoy on the Monday. A boat came to take the men away.

Bellavista was loaded with iron ore. Tugs came to try and pull her off, but they were frightened to try it in case the weight of the cargo might give too much strain and pull the bottom out of her, as she was an old ship.

The ship's cat was given to the ones at Kimbland. *Bellavista* lay there pounded by heavy seas, until I think it was in October or early November that she broke up. I mind on that lobsters that were caught in that area were a rusty colour.

Clothes

Clothes were usually bought from catalogues. J. D. William and Oxendale had the most popular catalogues when I wa young. Nowadays there are many more to choose from.

We also had second hand frocks which our cousins in Edin burgh had outgrown. We did think we were well dressed whe we got a bonnie frock on. Youngins will not wear cast off gar ments today which older brothers or sisters have been wearing.

Men would wear long knitted drawers (*underpants*). M mother knitted them. They would have been kind of warm i Summer. They always need a good blow on the washing line t get them dried.

John o' Vestness was sowing oats on a warm sunny day. H had his breeks off – it was warm enough with his drawers Someone came along and John followed this man along th road yarning as far as Tirlo, well past North Rendall.

When I went to school we wore leather lacing boots. Whe the soles wore out my father put on new soles. If a hole came o the boot, a leather patch would be sown on. Longer ago ther was a John Foulis who made boots for his family out of hid with soles made of bain.

In the old days there was a washing day each week. Th boiler was filled with water and a fire lighted. The clothes ha been soaked overnight. The trousers would be scrubbed on scrubbing board using a scrubbing brush.

There were no washing machines or spin dryers. There was a wringer but clothes were mostly wrung by hand.

If it was too windy the clothes were put on the dyke. Stones were laid to hold them or they were pegged to the stack net and would dry fine on the sheltered side. There are no stacks now – everything is silaged in a pit or in big round bales wrapped in plastic.

Davina o' Maybo left her washing out one night. In the morning when her man opened the door, he shouted "lass thee claes are all at the door". Her bloomers had been tied at both legs and stuffed wi' straw and for a head a kale stock was stuck in the top and tied and then tied to the door. The next day, Davina was burning kelp and Minnie o' Clestrain came along and Davina was telling her the story whit the boys had done. Minnie could not help laughing. So Davina says "it's no been the boys - it's been you limmers o' lasses".

Water and Electricity

There is a well on the land of Midhouse. Before 1965 there was a hand pump at the well. We had a barrel on a water sledge. We would pump it full and the horse would bring it home. Kirkhouse and Hinsobrae used the same well. They would use a horse and cart to carry the water. Cott and Shorehouse had their own well. Where my grandmother was born, the well was so small you would have to use a jug to collect the water.

In the olden days, our coats would get wet as we carried buckets of water to the beasts. In winter the water would freeze and we would have icicles hanging from our coats. Kimbland also used the well – a long way to carry buckets. Willie and someone else once carried pails up to Kimbland and lost them at the top of the brae.

The water scheme was put on in 1965. The well was made much bigger and it was such a good spring that it could serve four houses: Cott, Midhouse, Shorehouse and Kimbland. The tank was built at Kimbland and a pipe was laid from the well to the tank. The south and middle of the isle are on a different scheme with three wells connected to provide them with water. What an improvement when the water came on tap compared to carrying it in buckets for cooking.

Electricity

In 1980 electricity was brought to the island. What an improvement from box lanterns and Tilley lamps! Just to put on a switch is great and we miss it so much when we get a power cut. With the very strong wind, something can go wrong and sometimes most of the islands are cut off. But the Hydro engineers are very good at getting fixed as soon as possible. The Hydro engineers do not have it easy, having to climb the poles in all weathers.

Before the electricity supply came, most houses had a generator but they were restricted as to the amount of electricity we could use. Basically we got lights, an electric blanket and a TV. Some houses have kept their generators to use when the Hydro fails.

Earlier still, some houses had windchargers. These were fixed to the lum and provided the first form of electric light. We did not have one of them at Midhouse.

Water on tap and electricity were the two things that made such a difference to folk on Papay. Washing machines and spin dryers made washing much easier. Today washing machines are automatic but clothes still need to be dried outside although some have tumble dryers so that clothes are dry and ready for the airing cupboard.

SWRI group, undated.

Clubs and Associations

Women's Guild

The Women's Guild was formed in 1945 and when we had a minister his wife was president. We met once a month and sometimes we had a speaker. Occasionally, we had the male voice choir from Westray.

In 1970 we celebrated our 25th anniversary social on Friday 16th October. The President Mrs Cooper welcomed all present. The social took the form of an open meeting with five of the founder members present, Mrs Hourston, Mrs Miller, Mrs Milne, Mrs Rendall and Mrs Stanger.

Guild members took part in the programme. According to the programme, '*vocal musical items were rendered by Mrs Cooper, Mrs Cursiter and Miss Harcus. Taking part in readings and dialogues were Mrs Rendall, Mrs Stanger, Miss Harcus and Miss Sinclair.*' I was the 'Miss Harcus'.

There was a birthday cake which was cut by Mrs Rendall, a former President. Mr Groat from Longhope spoke in appreciation of what had been done by so many to make the evening a success. Mr Groat was formerly from Quoys in Papay.

For a time we visited Westray one year and they visited the next year until our numbers got fewer and not so easy to entertain a much bigger group. Our older members had passed on. The Guild was stopped in 1996.

S.W.R.I.

The Scottish Woman's Rural Institute was formed in 1927 and carried on until 1994. By that time there were too few members to keep it going.

There was always a welcome cup of tea at the meetings. Sometimes we would have a speaker. In March we had the bulb show and in the early days there were no cars so the meeting was usually held when the moon was bright. The bulb show was in March so the daylight was longer, but we still had to carry the pots of bulbs to the school. Someone would be appointed to judge the bulbs. The pots of bulbs were then put in the Kirk and it being cool the flowers would keep bright for a while.

We also had baking competitions and demonstrations anc
various other programmes.

The boys were always outside the school where we met. One
night they caught a drake from Daybreak and slipped it in at the
door to liven up the meeting. I was not old enough to go, sc
missed the night the drake walked in.

The Silver Jubilee was held in 1952. The Westray S.W.R.I
were invited and a good night was held. The Golden Jubilee wa.
held in 1977, the Westray branch joined us again for the celebra-
tion.

St Tredwall Model Yacht Club

The club was formed in the early 1930s. William Traill o
Holland and Mackie Grieve were among the first ones who or-
ganised the sailing. I mind William Traill had a walking stick
with a seat attached and he would stick it in the ground and sa
watching the yachts sailing.

Willie Cursiter and John Cursiter of Charleston and Tom
Miller of Whitehowe were among the first contestants.

The yachts were sailed on Christmas Day. A football match
was played on New Years Day between the north end men anc
the Sooth end men. The football game was held on the links o
Whitelooms.

The Christmas Say sailing was held for a number of years
and then changed to July. That continued until the last sailing
on the 20th July 1996.

A dance was held in the school on the night and prizes handed out to the winners.

Youth Club

The Youth Club was formed in 1949. There were 23 members when the first meeting took place on Tuesday 26th of April that year with John Cursiter as President. The club met almost every week. In those days the first part of the evening was spent playing games and after a break for tea there were some dances. The minutes of the first meeting record that Bill Irvine provided music on the fiddle.

People were invited to give talks. A Mr. Woodhead was invited to 1st November meeting that year and he talked about his experiences as a Japanese prisoner of war in Hong Kong.

The following year, among many other activities, the minutes record that the club held a picnic on the Papay Holm on the 1st of August. The weather conditions were not very good but they left the pier for the Holm in motor boats. The rain stopped and the club apparently spent a lovely evening on the Holm.

On the 12th of June 1951, no fewer than 41 members and their friends went to the Inter-Island Sports Day on Stronsay.

The Youth Club carried on and is still in existence.

Lifeboat Guild

The Lifeboat Guild was formed in 1954 and is still going. Over the years, we have had various functions, barbecues, coffee mornings, sales and house-to-house collections – all to raise money for the RNLI. Before Christmas we have a 'pot luck' supper when Santa comes to give the children their toys. At the end of January, the Lifeboat Guild hold a Burns Supper. Any profit left for the functions, after expenses are paid, all goes to the Lifeboat Guild. Although the isle is small we have raised a lot of money over the years.

In 1992, I was presented with a bronze statue of a lifeboat man. It was presented to me by the Duke of Kent at an evening function in Kirkwall. Maisie Rendall received a silver brooch.

Muckle Supper

Before the 1st World War workers at Holland had a Muckle Supper when the harvest work was finished. That was in Mrs Petrie's time. She had a big meal for the workers and anyone who had helped. Mrs Petrie said "Eat up noo for it it'll be all you get."

I do not know what year the island Muckle Supper would have started but it has been held for as long as I can remember. It is still held when the harvest is finished – in most places it is called 'harvest home'. Papay keeps the old tradition going and there's no reason for Papay to change it – it will always be the Muckle Supper.

There's plenty of food: soup, Holmie mutton, clapshot, jellies and ice cream. The Holmie mutton is boiled or roasted. Two sheep or maybe more were needed

There was a big number going then, and we usually had a programme of entertainment but numbers have been few in recent years. In the past we had members of the Stromness Drama Club who did the entertainment and it was very good.

The Muckle Supper was held in the school but now it is held in Beltane House. One year so many came that extra tables had to be found for the school.

There were times when the Muckle Supper date was the same as *Children in Need* and we would have something special to raise money for the charity.

Beach at Bothican

Lammas Picnic

Before the Second World War a picnic was held one year on the hill north of Bewan. A dance was held in Bewan's barn with music by Willie Cursiter on the button key accordion and Tom Hourston and Donald Mackay on the fiddle.

The following year, the picnic was held at Bothican with a dance in Charleston's barn. The Lammas picnic was a picnic for all the folk of the isle. A good time was spent at the picnic playing games and having races.

The picnics were stopped when the war began and never started up again.

When I went tae the school we always had a picnic when the school closed for the summer holidays. I mind that one year we were hoeing the tatties and my father said the tatties had to be finished before we got leave to go to the picnic. Sometimes ones would come from Westray for the isle's picnic.

Going to the Kirk, c. 1958 (Outside Papay School)

Left-to-right: John David Harcus, Thomas Hourston, Annie Flett, Maggie Drever, Anna Margaret Harcus, Mima Drever, Margaret Rendall, Wilma Rendall.

Kirk Socials

The Kirk social was usually held in March. It was a good night, we had singing, duets, quartets, solos and congregation singing, readings from anyone willing to provide for the programme. My sister Jess and myself would sing a duet, both of us singing soprano. Mrs Cooper would sing a solo and there would be a men's chorus from Tammie o' Whitelooms, Johnnie o' Cott, Willie Cursiter and Billy Miller. Mr Cooper would join in.

Tea was also provided when George Drever had the shop at Schoolplace or the east shop as it was called. He had a boiler in an outhoose and the boiler was filled wi' water and sometimes depending on the airt o wind it would take longer to boil. When the tea was ready a white hankie was put at the door so that the minister would ken that was the signal the tea was ready. I remember one time the boiler took longer so Tammo o' Skennist came tae the door and shouted "the tea's no ready yet" so the programme continued until the tea was ready. Sandwiches and cream cookies were handed around on trays and you got a bag with fancies and a biscuit or two. When the contents of the bag were eaten the pokie would be blown up and burst. Later, to save the bangs, the corner would be cut out on the pokie.

It was a struggle to get atween the seats wi' the pots o' tea. The social was a special occasion and it would be a big congregation. At one social I recall that Jeanno Harcus said to my father "if you had not been there I would have been the oldest person there the night."

The social held in 1984 was a special occasion. It was in the school and Radio Orkney had recording gear and that year the choir sang *Joseph's Coat of Many Colours*. Michael Riches was staying on the isle then so he trained the choir and we had to sing fast. It was a lot of practising to get it right, but it was a good night.

St Boniface Kirkyard

Funerals

The main service was conducted at the house and a short service followed at the graveside. In the old days, the coffins were carried from the house to the kirkyard using the shortest route as there was not much fencing in those days.

The coffin was carried on bier trees with one man walking in front. By bier trees I mean three poles used to carry the coffin. The pole in the middle was longest. The procession would stop every five minutes. The nearest relatives would take the first shift and then six more men would take over. I think it was usually Jimmy Foulis, who lived at Dykeside, who walked in front. He would turn around and face the coffin while the men changed. The changes would be carried on until they arrived at the graveside. The nearest relatives would have the last shift. The men wore black ties, black caps and black or navy coloured suits.

I remember two funerals on one day in 1940. My grand-mother Jessie Ross (her married name was Burgess) died at about the age of 85. She had moved from Sunnibraes so she was taken from Midhouse. Her funeral went from Midhouse to St Boniface and then Alan Hourston's grandfather, James Hourston, was taken from Whitelooms.

Last resting place at St Boniface

The year before, Maggie Rendall's funeral went from Blossom. They walked from Blossom and when they came to th road below Daybreak, instead of keeping to the road up pas Holland, they crossed over the brae of Skennest and across th land to Kirkhouse. Everyone was supposed to carry their ga masks but the men from Vestness left theirs hanging on a pos as soon as they were out of sight from their women folk.

Coffins were made on Papay by James Miller of Peatwel and Thomas Groat of South Rendall. Later James Rendall o Cuppin and John Rendall made them. Near relations of the deceased usually dug the grave.

In those days women did not attend funerals. They waite in the house until the minister and the nearest relatives cam back for tea.

If a body was found from the sea, they would bury it nea where it was found. I mind a grave at the bottom of the roa from Midhouse, to the right side. There were flags there. Joh Rendall told me that there were also graves at Cuppin. There i tale of burials at Kirk o'Hoo in the very old days. I mind wha looked like a doorway there.

If the coffin came from Kirkwall on the steamer the servic would be held where the boat came ashore before proceeding t the graveyard where another short service would be held. The first funeral service from the Kirk was in 1955 and nowadays funerals are either from the Kirk or the Gospel Hall.

Maggie outside Midhouse

Around the island

In this section I will take you around the houses of Papay as they were when I was younger. I remember some folk better than others, and I cannot claim to remember them all. Where possible, I have put their dates of birth and death.

*We start at **Midhouse**, where I live. Taking the east road from Midhouse and heading north we soon come to Shorehouse.*

Shorehouse

Shorehouse was a 'but-and-ben' with a closet in between. The but-end was where they would cook and sleep in a box bed. The east end would have a ben-end and closet. Most houses had a but-end and a ben-end and closet – the box beds made the partitions and the closet was the small room between.

There were three living there when I first mind: Geordie (George Hewison, 1885-1943), his wife Bella (Isabella, c. 1890-1973) and her brother Johnnie (John D. Mackay). Then Willie, Geordie's nephew, his wife Bab (Barbara) and David Hewison came and worked the farm for eighteen years between 1958 and 1977 before going back to Westray. For a long time, the house was used by the student ministers who came each summer.

Further north along the east road we come to a working farm:

Cott

Cott was unusual in that it was first built on a North-South line rather than East-West, like most of the other houses on the isle. I mind Annie (1886-1955) and her brother Willie Drever (1875-1944) and his wife Maggie (a Hourston from Vestness, 1879-1957). At one time Willie and Maggie were going to Leith by boat and Willie left the cabin but could not remember the number. Speaking to one of the crew, he said: "I'm lost me wife and me money." But obviously he found them again. Willie and Maggie had one boy, Johnnie (1911-1976), who married Mima (Jemima Bain) from Westray. She died in 2001. They had three daughters: Margaret, Annie and Wilma.

Continuing northwards along the east road we find a collection of buildings which are North and South Via.

South Via

My mother's brother, Willie Burgess (1882-1969), lived here with his wife Nellie (1891-1971) and thirteen children: Margery, Benjy, Jessie, Nanny, Duncan, George, Jean, Nelly, Jimmy, Addie, Olive, Billy and Johnny. This was a small house with not much room for so many children, although the oldest had moved away before the youngest were born. Two (George and Billy) died in childhood and the others eventually settled in Kirkwall, Edinburgh, Shetland and Australia.

North Via

This was made up of two houses. The east house was a but-and-ben and a closet. The west house was just a but-end and a closet. Willie Mackay (1902-1967) and his sister Anno (Ann Eileen, 1900-1981) lived in the east end with their parents William Mackay (1870-1952) and Hellen or Ellen (nee Drever, 1864-1933). John Drever (1861-1931) and his wife Annie (nee Traill, 1859-1936) lived in the west end. John was a fisherman and Annie a midwife. They had a daughter but she died in infancy.

The road turns to the west above North Via but directly northwards you see Stripes and Ness.

Stripes

Stripes was a but-and-ben and a small closet. Stewart Groat lived at Stripes and married Isobel (nee Rendall), John o'Holland's sister. They eventually moved to Clestrain in the 1950s. Stripes was used as a brethren meeting place and was vacant for a number of years.

Ness

I mind two sisters, Kirsty (Christina, 1865-1941) and Mimo (Jemima, 1863-1934) Drever and their niece Mary Ann Miller. That was three at Ness. Ness would have been a but-and-ben and a closet. Mimo had heart problems and used to say: "Wi' the hearty trouble you were here the day and away the morn." Mary Ann married Jamie o' Vestness and moved there.

Then Willie Groat (c. 1881-1947), a seaman who had been brought up at Ness by Kirsty and Mimo, moved back from Faray with Jessie Ann (nee Hume, 1882-1861) and two of their family – came to Papay about 1935. They were first in Stripes and then moved to the Ness around 1950, after the auld women died. Stewart, their oldest son came later to work the farm. There was also a daughter Annie who moved to Kirkwall.

Northwards along the shore you meet the end of the road at the north hill. Hundland and Bewan are here.

Hundland

Johnnie Seatter (1861-1928) and Katie (Catherine, nee Foulis, 1869-1961) lived here with their daughter Jenny (Janet Ann, 1905-1946). Jenny married Willie Gray from Vola but they had no family. Willie married Chrissie Groat (Christine, c. 1916-1990) and they had two boys, Johnnie and William. William went to Kirkwall. Johnnie married Kathy and stayed on the isle with their son Martin before they left for mainland Orkney as well.

Kimbland

I mind Andrew Groat (1876-1952) and Pheemo (nee Allan, 1883-1971) and their family: Jean Ann, Stewart, Mary and Willie. Andrew and my father spent many an hour yarning, sometimes in the graveyard. Andrew was chief officer of the Coastguard on Papay, a job later passed on to Willie. Kimbland was a but-and-ben and closet until it was extended in the 1960's.

Hinsobrae

I mind Willie Irvine (c. 1840-1928) and Mary (nee Hourston, c. 1851-1932), his second wife. There is a story about Willie going to St Ann's Kirk. The dog followed Willie to the Kirk and he came right up to the choir. Willie took him by the scruff of the neck and said "though his no need o' the gospel" and put the dog outside. I think it was Willie that said "I'm gaen three score years and ten on two legs and noo I'm no ashamed to take a third leg" - meaning his walking stick.

There was a man going around selling clothes and said to Mary that he had outsize ones. Mary said all her boys were outsize! They were all tall. Two of them were killed in the first World War. Johnnie became a sailor and Willie went to Canada and then Liverpool.

Johnnie Irvine was in the Navy in the 1st World War. One day a German submarine surfaced. He took aim and fired and sank the submarine - he hit right on the periscope. My father asked how far he would have been away. They were outside Hinso, so he said from where they were to the Kern Head at the sooth end of the Holm. That would be about a mile.

Geordie (1893-1972) also went to Canada and fought with the Canadian army in France during World War 1. Afterwards he stayed with his mother and worked as a gardener for Willie Traill at Holland. Then he married and farmed at Hookin before settling at the Links. Jamie married Annie (nee Rendall) and they lived in the west end.

During the first World War, a Zeppelin flew over Papay. My father and his friends were having a yarn and my father says: "it flew between Kimbland and Hinso". Johnnie o' Hinso says: "Lord forga they Johnnie o' mothers for it flew right ower Willie Hume's lum". Willie Hume’s lum (*chimney*) was at Kirkhouse.

Kirkhouse

The west end of Kirkhouse was a but-end and a small bed-room. I mind Willie Hume staying there – he was married to Fanny (Frances) Rendall from Westray. She was his second wife, his first being Jane (or Jean) Groat - the daughter of David Groat of Quoys - who had passed away in 1909. Willie had three girls with Jane but they all had TB and died at the ages of 17, 15 and 11. I can’t remember what Willie looked like but Fanny had a pleasant look and grey hair and, like all the older women then, wore a shawl similar to what we might wear as a headsquare. Dr Cursiter said Willie called her first ‘mam’, then ‘bairn’ and then ‘buddo’. And as long as Willie lived, it was ‘buddo’. He gave eve-ryone a nickname.

Willie was a coastguard and had medals for the ‘City of Lin-coln’ and ‘Badger’ rescues. Willie Hume had a problem wi’ his waterworks. He had a walk every night as far as the memorial and that helped.

My father and a few cronies were having a yarn outside at Kirkhouse. Willie Hume, who gave nearly everyone a nickname, saw someone walking along the shore road and says "that's auld Pin". He suddenly minded on that her son was there and he says "no, no - it's Auntie May o' the Green".

Another story about Willie Hume: he built a peedie (*small*) porch at the door. One day he was in the graveyard and he pulled up his grandmother's gravestone and said it had stood there long enough. So he took it home and put it for a roof to the peedie porch.

Willie died on the 18th of August, 1931 aged 76. Fanny lived on until after the war.

Robbo Rendall was short and stout and getting bald. Robbo had married Annie Groat from Westray, a sweet looking woman, and they moved into the west end of Kirkhouse sometime around 1930. She had a daughter. It would have been four at Kirkhouse.

The daughter, Jessie Ann, married Wallace Sandison – they were married in Kirkwall, then came to Papay for a wedding party at Kirkhouse. I went with Mary Groat of Kimbland to the party. That was over 60 years ago. A good night was spent with games and dances in the barn. The barn is no longer there.

Annie Groat was Mary's auntie and we were always going along there together so that Robbo would say 'here's the Siamese twins.'

Robbo and Annie Groat died just before the war.

Knap of Howar in the 1940s

Further south along the west road, passing the airfield and the War Memorial, we come to Holland.

Holland

Willie Traill stayed at Holland House until he died in 1944. He had excavated the Knap of Howar. Eventually, the house and land were taken over by Johnnie (died 1979) and Maggie Hourston (nee Stout, died 1993) together with their daughter and son-in-law, Annie Jean and John Rendall from Cuppin. Johnnie Hourston came from Windywalls and Maggie from Westray.

Ivy Cottage (now Micklegarth)

Jamie Bremner and his wife Annie Brown stayed in Ivy Cottage. They were managers of Holland. When they left, Abby Brown (Annie's brother) and his wife Jessie took on the management. After them came Henry Rendall with his wife Emily (another Brown sister) and then John Scott and Katie between 1941 and 1945. Johnny Hourston lived at Ivy Cottage until he and John Rendall bought the mansion house.

Newhouses

There were six 'new houses' built mainly for Holland servants. Each had two rooms – not much for a family but they survived. I remember Mary Miller at No. 1. She died in 1949. John Rendall and Annie Jean were at No. 1 until they moved to Holland House in 1955. Mimmie Thomson, William Cursiter of Charleston's widow, stayed at No. 2. Peedie Johnno Rendall and Doddo were in No. 2 before they moved on, as were Robbie Hume and Isabel who went to the Falklands. Mackie Grieve, Willie Traill's gardener lived at No. 3. Peedie Geordo Rendall, Mimo and family were in No. 4. Jamie Hume and his wife Jessie Mowatt were in no. 5. Some of the same folk were in No. 6 at other times.

The houses became derelict and were converted into Beltane House where the shop and guest house are now. **Alsker** was built nearby as an entirely new house for the manager of Belatane.

May Cottage

Dr. Dow came from Westray after he retired and was joined later by his daughter, Marion Cooper, and her husband Sydney (1919-1979). Sydney Cooper was a lay missionary and Mrs Cooper was a mathematics and science teacher on Westray.

Taking the road down towards the old pier we come to the Manse, Bilboa, Dykeside, Morven House, School Place and the Kirk of St Ann's.

The Manse (now St. Tredwell's House)

The Manse was a big house with four bedrooms, bathroom and kitchen. Several ministers stayed there, including Sydney and Marion Cooper. Later the Manse was used by the men building the new pier at Moclett.

Bilboa

There was old Tommy Burgar (born 1850-1936) and Maggie Jean (c. 1886-1970). He had emigrated to the USA but returned to Bilboa. Young Tommy Burgar (1876-1961) and Geordie (died 1970) were both in New Zealand for some time. Bilboa was sold to Stewart and Lizzie Gray from Vola. Lizzie died in 1982.

Dykeside

I mind Jimmo Foulis (1885-1936), Jeanno Hume, Jessie and Johnny Hourston and their family. Rita married Jock (John) Hume. Rita's uncle Jamie came to stay at Dykeside.

Jimmo Foulis always went to the Kirk for the evening service at six o'clock. He would look at his watch and say "it's straight handles again."

Morven House

It was built in 1926 for the island doctor. Then it was Dr. McPhail who married Ian Cursiter from Gairbolls. They went for a year to Africa but came back to Papay and she got the doctor's post again. When they left in 1945 they went to Colonsay. After that none of the doctors stayed long.

School Place

First I mind Geordie Drever (1869-1948) and his wife Betty (Elizabeth, nee Mackay, c. 1865-1939). He had a shop there. Then Peedie Geordie Rendall (1901-1955) and Mimo (Tomima, nee Hourston, c. 1899-1959) took over the shop.

Beyond the Kirk we find the Schoolhouse and Daybreak.

Schoolhouse

Maggie Shields and her sister Chris were there – Maggie was the teacher for a number of years. Then William Maclean and his mother came. He married and later moved to another school. Ian Young and his wife Grace and boys were there between 1952 and 1954. James McGhee came in 1954 with his daughter Elizabeth and housekeeper, Alice Miller, whom he married. He died suddenly in 1960. Gordon Riddell was there between 1961 and 1966 as teacher and minister. Then Edith Sinclair came between 1970 and 1982. Finally, Christine Hopkins stayed at the house before moving to Quoys.

Daybreak

My uncle, Andrew Miller (1900-1976), and auntie Jessi
(nee Burgess, 1900-1985) lived there with his father Johnni
Miller (1862-1931).

Beyond Daybreak the road divides. One fork takes us pas Nouster, the ruins of Sunnybraes and Bayview to the old pier.

Nouster

I mind Tammie and Betty Miller and their daughter Mar
who married Peedie Robbie Rendall. Robbie's uncle – anothe
Robbie Rendall (died 1954) - from Blossom came to live there
Peedie Robbie was a blacksmith and had a forge on the lean-t
at the east side of the coal store that belonged to the Papay Co
operative Society. Nouster was given an upper storey in th
1920's. After old Robbie and his wife died, Nannie Stainge
from Breckaskaill came to be Peedie Robbie's housekeeper
Peedie Robbie died in 1980 and Nannie in 1985.

Sunnybraes

Sunnybraes was just a but-and-ben. My grandparents, Ben
jamin and Jessie Burgess, lived here for a while. My grandfathe
died in 1925 but granny stayed at Sunnybraes until 1930 befor
she came to Midhouse to live with us. Big Dave Drever (1861
1936) from Bewan stayed here between 1930 and 1934 and the
went back to Bewan. He had emigrated to Collingwood in Can
ada for a while in the 1920's.

Bayview

Mary and Robbie Rendall had a small shop here.

Turning left at the Kelp Store we turn north on the east road to Skennist, Maybo and Roadside.

Skennist

The house was heightened to include two upstairs bedrooms in 1904. Old John Drever (1857-1936) lived here with son Tommo (1897-1964) and Tommo's wife, Eddie (Edith, nee Corse). They had three children: Kathleen, Ruby and Jackie. There was also Tommo's sister Betty (c. 1930-1932) with her three: Bessie, John and Jim.

Maybo

Maybo is one of the oldest houses on Papay. I mind Davina (Margaret Davina, nee Drever, c. 1868-1950), Johnnie (John D. Mackay, born 1910) and Danny (Donald, 1893-1965). Davina had been married to John Mackay (1866-1914) who had come from Caithness and was once a servant at Holland. They had three sons in all but one (Thomas) had died young in 1915.

Danny married Maggie (Margaret Harcus, 1902-1983) from Gowrie and they had three: Tommy (1926-1997), Mina (1933-1991) and Ella (born 1934).

Johnnie was a teacher with a fine turn of phrase. He remarked about a meal that he had one time at the Manse that it was very tasty and adequate and a nice variety at the table – although not elaborate.

Once there were seven at Maybo, but now it is vacant. Tommy thought the couples (roof supports) were bad and the roof might collapse so he lived in a caravan before he died. Tommy kept in touch with visitors to Papay around the world. When he died on October 20 1997 he had already sent 80 Christmas cards abroad.

Roadside (also known as the Green)

Johnno Foulis (born 1868), also known as 'Jock o' the Green, was here with his wife Fanny (Frances, nee Lesley) and their daughters, Mary and Maggie.

We turn back to Daybreak now and take the fork leading to Links and Hookin.

Links

I remember Robbie Milne (1862-c. 1945) living here with his daughter Maggie (born 1887) and her son Johnnie. Geordie Irvine (born 1893), his wife Mary Ann (nee Hourston, born 1897) and son Bill moved to Links from Hookin in 1946. Bill married Addie (Andrina, nee Burgess) from South Via.

Hookin

I mind Fletts in it. Frank Flett (c. 1883-1966) married Annie Drever and went to Bewan. I think that Frank's father was Robert and the mother was Marjory. They moved to Westray. The mother stayed in bed all the winter and got up in summer. The Irvines were then in Hookin until 1946.

Looking north past Breckaskaill to Holland

Now we head back to Holland and take the road south, past *the new Fire Station and Telephone Exchange, to the junction at Breckaskaill.*

Breckaskaill

This was a but-and-ben and small closet. Tammie Hewison (1864-1942) and wife Mary (nee Miller, 1865-1940) stayed here with their daughter Nannie (died 1985 at Nouster). Nannie married Willie Stainger and when her parents and Willie died, Breckaskaill was sold to Geordie and Bella from Cuppin. They died in 1978 and 1979.

Turning west, we take the road to Backaskaill past Gairbolls and Edgeriggs.

Gairbolls

Gairbolls was originally a low house. Old David Cursiter died in 1935. His son, Ian Cursiter, married Dr. McPhaill and stayed at Morven House but worked the land at Gairbolls. His sister Nancy married Doddie Miller and lived at Backaskaill. My brother, Tommy and his wife Annie were at Gairbolls for a time when Tommy worked at Holland.

Edgeriggs

John Robertson (1872-1942) and his wife Elizabeth (nee Davidson, 1873-1956) lived there. He died in 1942 and she died in 1956. Their daughters Maggie and Lizzie both died in Kirkwall.

Elizabeth, or Betto o' Edgeriggs as she was known, was a character. One morning when the boat was going off to the steamer at Backaskaill, I think it was a doctor who said to her "'that's a bad cough you have got". She said "that's just a morning cough".

Lizzie took her mother into Kirkwall to stay wi' her when Betto was no longer able to be on her own. The minister came to visit her and said: " I'm glad, Mrs Robertson, you have come to civilization." She replied: " I hae come fae whar the folk are civilised but they're no civilised here!"

Backaskaill

Backaskaill was a shop named Groat and Miller. Davie Groat and Doddie Miller were half brothers. The shop had shelves on each side – not self-service – and there was no till to count the price of your messages (*goods*). The ones at the counter had to add up the total and look for the goods. Later the west end of the building was made into a kitchen and bathroom.

Doddie Miller married Nancy and they had two lasses. Doddie, Nancy and family left Papay and he went to work in Lyness. I'm not sure what year that was. I doubt that the shop would have provided a living for two families with two more shops on the island.

Davie married Lena from Moclett and her sister Jean worked to them. Davie and Jean had two girls. Jim Rendall worked there until Lena gave up the shop and he took it over. Jim, Margaret and the family moved there and kept it until 1980 when the Papay Community Co-op started up. The Post Office was still at Backaskaill until recently.

We return to the main road and head south again towards Peatwell, North Rendall, South Rendall and Whitehowe.

Peatwell

Peatwell was more than a but-and-ben. There was a passage from the back door with a room on the left side. On the right side was a kitchen, bedroom, bathroom and the west end used for a bedroom. Peatwell had four chimneys. My earliest recollection is of Mary (died 1948) and Jamie Miller (died 1948). Then Alec Davidson and his wife Mary were there before moving to Cambuslang. Alec was a joiner. When they left, Alec's sister Cissie and her father (died 1966) and mother (died 1955) bought the property and moved there in 1951.

Old North Rendall

North Rendall

Originally a but-and-ben but it has changed considerably. Robbie Rendall and Maggie Jean (nee Allan) lived there. They had a son, Johnny, who married Maggie Seatter from Westray and two daughters, Alice and Dorothy.

South Rendall

Tammie Groat (died 1950) and his wife Maggie were there. They had no family. May Gray was there for a while until she moved to Gayfield Cottage.

Whitehowe

Betty Miller was blind and Beeno, her son, married Maggie (nee Rendall). Betty's husband was drowned between Papay and Westray. Beeno died in 1966 and Maggie died in 1968 –

they had been married more than 60 years. They had two sons: Johnny and Tommo and a daughter Elizabeth. She died in 1931 and John died in 1928.

Tommo married Chrissie Groat and they had a son and daughter, Billy and Elizabeth. Tommo and Chrissie moved to Finstown.

There are several houses at the south of the island: Windywalls, Gayfield, Gayfield Cottage, Tredwall, Fairview, Charleston, Vestness, Vola, Southouse and Nistaben.

Windywalls

I remember Jock Hourston and Mary Jean. They had a son, Johnny, who was a servant at Holland. He married a Westray wife, Maggie Stout. Their daughter Mary Anne married Geordie Irvine and had a son, Bill.

Ronnie (died 1984) and Norah Babinou (died 1988) then came from Malaysia. Subsequently the house was bought by Rob and Fiona McNab, the island nurse.

Gayfield

I remember George (died 1956) and Jessie Rendall (died 1944). Jessie was a teacher and the couple had no family. I was never in Gayfield. It might have been a but-end and two bedrooms. The people that inherited it never did anything about the furniture so it has been left as it was in 1956. It is getting in a bad state now.

Gayfield Cottage

Jamie and Bell Thomson stayed here. Both died in 1939. Bell Thomson had St Vitus' Dance. When my sister and I were both young and going to Vestness we would run past Gayfield Cottage in case Bell Thomson came out. She would fling her arms around and that frightened us.

Georgie Rendall was a son of George Rendall of Tredwall. His wife, Margaret came from Blackburn in Lancashire. They married in 1946. Georgie was in the Merchant Navy, having left Papay in 1940 to join the 'Pole Star'. His ship was torpedoed. Georgie and other crew members were in a lifeboat for about two weeks suffering hot days and cold nights before they were rescued.

Tredwall

Geordie (died 1967) and Kitty Rendall (died 1966). Geordie and Kitty had a shop at Tredwall. Kitty taught in the school sometimes and Geordie did hiring and the 'school run'. They had two children, Geordie and Cathy who both left the island.

Fairview

Fairview is a modern house with two bedrooms, sitting room, kitchen and bathroom. It was built for Peggy Harcus but she died before it was completed.

Charleston

My sister Jess lived here with her husband Willie Cursiter. Willie's parents Johnny and Davina lived here before them.

Singling neeps at Vestness

Vestness

Tammie (died 1962) and Maggie Hourston (died 1964) lived at Vestness. Maggie was my Aunt and a Harcus. Before Uncle Tammie died Auntie Maggie became very forgetful and would wander away, always wanting to go home to Midhouse where she was born. After he died, we took her to live with us and she was never able to go back to Vestness. They had no family.

Southouse

Stewart (died 1940) and Catherine Harcus (died 1925). Stewart was a brother to my grandfather, Thomas Harcus. Stewart Harcus' son Timothy married May Gray. They had three lasses: Marjory, Kitty and Peggy. Kitty nursed in Edinburgh before she went to Canada. She came back to Papay to look after her mother. Peggy was a sewing maid at the Balfour Hospital. When she left her job at the Balfour Peggy came back to Papay to be school cook and was there until she retired.

Marjory (died 1987) and Jimmy Hume (died 1966) had a family of five: Timothy, John David, Stewart, Kenneth and Marion. John David stayed at Southouse; Stewart went to Shetland; Timothy, Kenneth and Marion went to Kirkwall.

Vola

Johnny Gray worked the farm and went creel fishing. His wife, Maggie, was a cousin of my father's. They had three sons: Johnny, Willie and Stewart. Johnny was a sailing Captain. He married Teenie Corse and moved to Stromness. Willie married Jenny Seatter and moved to Hundland.

After Johnny Gray was no longer able, Stewart worked the farm at Vola. He married Lizzie Hume and stayed at Vola until they bought Bilboa.

Nistaben

Willie Gray and his wife Georgina lived here. They had one son, Johnny, and three daughters: Magie, May and Doddo. Doddo married Peedie Johnnie Rendall who was a servant at Holland.

Heading back to the road for the new pier at Moclett, we pass the road to Sheepheight and Moclett itself.

Sheepheight (now Hazedale)

Jamie Davidson (died 1966) and his wife Mimie (died 1955) stayed in one part of the house. Their daughter Cissie stayed with them. There were three sons: Johnny, Jamie and Alec. Johnny married Betty Bain from Westray and they lived in the other part of the house. They also had three sons and a daughter: John, Alec, Jim and Robina.

Moclett

Willie Burgar (died 1948) and his wife Maggie (died 1968) and two daughters stayed here. Willie and his wife moved to Backaskaill when they were no longer fit to work the farm.

Heading north across the land we come to our final two houses, Blossom and Cuppin.

Blossom

Maggie (died 1939) and Jeremiah Rendall (died 1922). It was a very bad road from Blossom but Maggie, Jeremiah and their son Robbie would come to the Kirk. When the service was at 6 o'clock it would be dark in the winter. Maggie would say that she "just took me lantern wi' me" – it was a double cell light, much fainter than the big square battery light we use now.

Cuppin

Geordie and Bella Rendall stayed here with their family: Mary Ann, Isabella and John. Mary Ann left the island to work. She married Tony Laughton and lived at The Tower in Orphir.

Spinning at Blossom

Threshing the crop at Cuppin

Isabella went to Kirkwall to work but came back to Papay and married Stewart Groat. They stayed at Stripes but when Clestrain came up for sale they bought it and moved there. John went to work at Holland farm, later marrying Annie Jean.

Jammo Rendall, a brother of Geordie, stayed at Cuppin. He built boats and also made the coffins. He moved to Breckaskaill with Geordie and Bella and Cuppin was sold to Johnnie Rendall of North Rendall. Bella's mother, Mary Miller, left Cuppin in 1922 or 1923 and stayed at No. 1 Newhouses. She died in 1949.